THE ORDER OF MASS

IN LATIN AND ENGLISH

The New English Translation

All booklets are published thanks to the generous support of the members of the Catholic Truth Society

CATHOLIC TRUTH SOCIETY
PUBLISHERS TO THE HOLY SEE

Contents

Ordo Missæ cum Populo

Contents

The Order of Mass with a Congregation

Ordo Missæ Cum Populo

The Introductory Rites

Before Mass begins, the people gather in a spirit of recollection, preparing for their participation in the Mass.

All stand during the entrance procession.

Sign of the Cross

After the Entrance Chant, the Priest and the faithful sign themselves with the Sign of the Cross:

Priest: In nómine Patris, et Fílii, et Spíritus Sancti.

Response: Amen.

Greeting

The Priest greets the people, with one of the following:

1. Pr. Grátia Dómini nostri Iesu Christi, et cáritas Dei, et communicátio Sancti Spíritus sit cum ómnibus vobis.

R. Et cum spíritu tuo.

2. Pr. Grátia vobis et pax a Deo Patre nostro et Dómino Iesu Christo.

R. Et cum spíritu tuo.

The Order of Mass with a Congregation

The Introductory Rites

Before Mass begins, the people gather in a spirit of recollection, preparing for their participation in the Mass.

All stand during the entrance procession.

Sign of the Cross

After the Entrance Chant, the Priest and the faithful sign themselves with the Sign of the Cross:

Priest: In the name of the Father, and of the Son, and of the Holy Spirit.

Response: Amen.

Greeting

The Priest greets the people, with one of the following:

1. Pr. The grace of our Lord Jesus Christ,
and the love of God,
and the communion of the Holy Spirit
be with you all.

R. And with your spirit.

2. Pr. Grace to you and peace from God our Father
and the Lord Jesus Christ.

R. And with your spirit.

3. Pr. Dóminus vobíscum.

R. Et cum spíritu tuo.

The Priest, or a Deacon, or another minister, may very briefly introduce the faithful to the Mass of the day.

Penitential Act

There are three forms of the Penitential Act which may be chosen from as appropriate. From time to time on Sundays, especially in Easter Time, instead of the customary Penitential Act, the blessing and sprinkling of water may take place as a reminder of Baptism. Each Penitential Act begins with the invitation to the faithful by the Priest:

Pr. Fratres, agnoscámus peccáta nostra,
ut apti simus ad sacra mystéria celebránda.

A brief pause for silence follows.
Then one of the following forms is used:

---

1. Confíteor Deo omnipoténti et vobis, fratres,
quia peccávi nimis
cogitatióne, verbo, ópere et omissióne:

(and, striking their breast, they say:)
mea culpa, mea culpa, mea máxima culpa.

3. Pr. The Lord be with you.
R. And with your spirit.
The Priest, or a Deacon, or another minister, may very briefly introduce the faithful to the Mass of the day.

Penitential Act

There are three forms of the Penitential Act which may be chosen from as appropriate. From time to time on Sundays, especially in Easter Time, instead of the customary Penitential Act, the blessing and sprinkling of water may take place as a reminder of Baptism. Each Penitential Act begins with the invitation to the faithful by the Priest:

Pr. Brethren (brothers and sisters),
let us acknowledge our sins,
and so prepare ourselves to celebrate the sacred mysteries.
A brief pause for silence follows.
Then one of the following forms is used:

---

1. I confess to almighty God
and to you, my brothers and sisters,
that I have greatly sinned,
in my thoughts and in my words,
in what I have done and in what I have failed to do,
(and, striking their breast, they say:)
through my fault, through my fault,
through my most grievous fault;

Ideo precor beátam Mariám semper Vírginem,
omnes Angelos et Sanctos,
et vos, fratres, oráre pro me
ad Dóminum Deum nostrum.

---

2. Pr. Miserére nostri, Dómine.
R. Quia peccávimus tibi.
Pr. Osténde nobis, Dómine, misericórdiam tuam.
R. Et salutáre tuum da nobis.

Invocations naming the gracious works of the Lord may be made, as in the example below:

3. Pr. Qui missus es sanáre contrítos corde: Kýrie, eléison.
R. Kýrie, eléison.

Pr. Qui peccatóres vocáre venísti: Christe, eléison.
R. Christe, eléison.

Pr. Qui ad déxteram Patris sedes, ad interpellándum pro nobis: Kýrie, eléison.
R. Kýrie, eléison.

The absolution by the Priest follows:

Pr. Misereátur nostri omnípotens Deus
et, dimíssis peccátis nostris,
perdúcat nos ad vitam ætérnam.
R. Amen.

therefore I ask blessed Mary ever-Virgin,
all the Angels and Saints,
and you, my brothers and sisters,
to pray for me to the Lord our God.

---

2. Pr. Have mercy on us, O Lord.
R. For we have sinned against you.
Pr. Show us, O Lord, your mercy.
R. And grant us your salvation.

Invocations naming the gracious works of the Lord may be made, as in the example below:

3. Pr. You were sent to heal the contrite of heart:
Lord, have mercy. *Or:* Kýrie, eléison.
R. Lord, have mercy. *Or:* **Kýrie, eléison.**
Pr. You came to call sinners:
Christ, have mercy. *Or:* Christe, eléison.
R. Christ, have mercy. *Or:* **Christe, eléison.**
Pr. You are seated at the right hand of the Father to intercede for us:
Lord, have mercy. *Or:* Kýrie, eléison.
R. Lord, have mercy. *Or:* **Kýrie, eléison.**

The absolution by the Priest follows:

Pr. May almighty God have mercy on us,
forgive us our sins,
and bring us to everlasting life.
R. Amen.

The Kýrie, eléison *(*Lord, have mercy*) invocations follow, unless they have just occurred.*

Pr. Kýrie, eléison. **R. Kýrie, eléison.**
Pr. Christe, eléison. **R. Christe, eléison.**
Pr. Kýrie eléison. **R. Kýrie, eléison.**

The Gloria

On Sundays (outside of Advent and Lent), Solemnities and Feast Days, this hymn is either sung or said:

Glória in excélsis Deo
et in terra pax homínibus bonæ voluntátis.

Laudámus te,
benedícimus te,
adorámus te,
glorificámus te,
grátias ágimus tibi propter magnam glóriam tuam,
Dómine Deus, Rex cæléstis,
Deus Pater omnípotens.

Dómine Fili Unigénite, Iesu Christe,
Dómine Deus, Agnus Dei, Fílius Patris,
qui tollis peccáta mundi, miserére nobis;
qui tollis peccáta mundi, súscipe deprecatiónem nostram.
Qui sedes ad déxteram Patris, miserére nobis.

Quóniam tu solus Sanctus, tu solus Dóminus,
tu solus Altíssimus,

The Kýrie, eléison *(*Lord, have mercy*) invocations follow, unless they have just occurred.*

Pr. Lord, have mercy. **R. Lord, have mercy.**
Pr. Christ, have mercy. **R. Christ, have mercy.**
Pr. Lord, have mercy. **R. Lord, have mercy.**

The Gloria

On Sundays (outside of Advent and Lent), Solemnities and Feast Days, this hymn is either sung or said:

**Glory to God in the highest,
and on earth peace to people of good will.**

**We praise you,
we bless you,
we adore you,
we glorify you,
we give you thanks for your great glory,
Lord God, heavenly King,
O God, almighty Father.**

**Lord Jesus Christ, Only Begotten Son,
Lord God, Lamb of God, Son of the Father,
you take away the sins of the world, have mercy on us;
you take away the sins of the world, receive our prayer;
you are seated at the right hand of the Father,
have mercy on us.**

**For you alone are the Holy One,
you alone are the Lord,**

Iesu Christe, cum Sancto Spíritu: in glória Dei Patris. Amen.

When this hymn is concluded, the Priest, says:

Pr. Orémus.

And all pray in silence. Then the Priest says the Collect prayer, which ends:

R. Amen.

you alone are the Most High,
Jesus Christ,
with the Holy Spirit,
in the glory of God the Father.
Amen.

When this hymn is concluded, the Priest, says:

Pr. Let us pray.

And all pray in silence. Then the Priest says the Collect prayer, which ends:

R. Amen.

The Liturgy of the Word

By hearing the word proclaimed in worship, the faithful again enter into the unending dialogue between God and the covenant people.

First Reading

The reader goes to the ambo and proclaims the First Reading, while all sit and listen. The reader ends:

Verbum Dómini.

R. Deo grátias.

It is appropriate to have a brief time of quiet between readings as those present take the word of God to heart.

Psalm

The psalmist or cantor sings or says the Psalm, with the people making the response.

Second Reading

On Sundays and certain other days there is a second reading. It concludes with the same response as above.

Gospel

The assembly stands for the Gospel Acclamation. Except during Lent the Acclamation is:

R. Allelúia

During Lent the following forms are used:

R. Laus tibi, Christe, Rex ætérnæ glóriæ! *Or:*

R. Laus et honor tibi, Dómine Iesu! *Or:*

R. Glória et laus tibi, Christe! *Or:*

R. Glória tibi, Christe, Verbo Dei!

The Liturgy of the Word

By hearing the word proclaimed in worship, the faithful again enter into the unending dialogue between God and the covenant people.

First Reading

The reader goes to the ambo and proclaims the First Reading, while all sit and listen. The reader ends:

The word of the Lord.

R. **Thanks be to God.**

It is appropriate to have a brief time of quiet between readings as those present take the word of God to heart.

Psalm

The psalmist or cantor sings or says the Psalm, with the people making the response.

Second Reading

On Sundays and certain other days there is a second reading. It concludes with the same response as above.

Gospel

The assembly stands for the Gospel Acclamation. Except during Lent the Acclamation is:

R. **Alleluia**

During Lent the following forms are used:

R. **Praise to you, O Christ, king of eternal glory!** *Or:*

R. **Praise and honour to you, Lord Jesus!** *Or:*

R. **Glory and praise to you, O Christ!** *Or:*

R. **Glory to you, O Christ, you are the Word of God!**

At the ambo the Deacon, or the Priest says:

Pr. Dóminus vobíscum.

R. Et cum spíritu tuo.

Pr. Léctio sancti Evangélii secúndum N.,

He makes the Sign of the Cross on the book and, together with the people, on his forehead, lips, and breast.

R. Glória tibi, Dómine.

At the end of the Gospel:

Pr. Verbum Dómini.

R. Laus tibi, Christe.

The Homily

Then follows the Homily, which is preached by a Priest or Deacon on all Sundays and Holydays of Obligation. After a brief silence all stand.

The Creed

On Sundays and Solemnities, the Profession of Faith will follow. During Lent and Easter Time, the Apostles' Creed may be used.

The Niceno-Constantinopolitan Creed

Credo in unum Deum,
Patrem omnipoténtem,
factórem cæli et terræ,
visibílium ómnium et invisibílium.
Et in unum Dóminum Iesum Christum,
Fílium Dei Unigénitum,

At the ambo the Deacon, or the Priest says:

Pr. The Lord be with you.

R. And with your spirit.

Pr. A reading from the holy Gospel according to N.

He makes the Sign of the Cross on the book and, together with the people, on his forehead, lips, and breast.

R. Glory to you, O Lord.

At the end of the Gospel:

Pr. The Gospel of the Lord.

R. Praise to you, Lord Jesus Christ.

The Homily

Then follows the Homily, which is preached by a Priest or Deacon on all Sundays and Holydays of Obligation. After a brief silence all stand.

The Creed

On Sundays and Solemnities, the Profession of Faith will follow. During Lent and Easter Time, the Apostles' Creed may be used.

The Niceno-Constantinopolitan Creed

I believe in one God,
the Father almighty,
maker of heaven and earth,
of all things visible and invisible.

I believe in one Lord Jesus Christ,
the Only Begotten Son of God,

et ex Patre natum ante ómnia sǽcula.
Deum de Deo, lumen de lúmine,
Deum verum de Deo vero,
génitum, non factum, consubstantiálem Patri:
per quem ómnia facta sunt.
Qui propter nos hómines et propter nostram salútem
descéndit de cælis. *(all bow)*
Et incarnátus est de Spíritu Sancto
ex María Vírgine, et homo factus est.

Crucifíxus étiam pro nobis sub Póntio Piláto;
passus et sepúltus est,
et resurréxit tértia die, secúndum Scriptúras,
et ascéndit in cælum, sedet ad déxteram Patris.

Et íterum ventúrus est cum glória,
iudicáre vivos et mórtuos,
cuius regni non erit finis.

Et in Spíritum Sanctum, Dóminum et vivificántem:
qui ex Patre Filióque procédit.
Qui cum Patre et Fílio simul adorátur et conglorificátur:
qui locútus est per prophétas.

Et unam, sanctam, cathólicam et apostólicam Ecclésiam.
Confíteor unum baptísma in remissiónem peccatórum.
Et exspécto resurrectiónem mortuórum,
et vitam ventúri sǽculi. Amen.

born of the Father before all ages.
God from God, Light from Light,
true God from true God,
begotten, not made, consubstantial with the Father;
through him all things were made.
For us men and for our salvation
he came down from heaven, *(all bow)*
and by the Holy Spirit was incarnate of the Virgin Mary,
and became man.

For our sake he was crucified under Pontius Pilate,
he suffered death and was buried,
and rose again on the third day
in accordance with the Scriptures.
He ascended into heaven
and is seated at the right hand of the Father.
He will come again in glory
to judge the living and the dead
and his kingdom will have no end.

I believe in the Holy Spirit, the Lord, the giver of life,
who proceeds from the Father and the Son,
who with the Father and the Son is adored and glorified,
who has spoken through the prophets.

I believe in one, holy, catholic and apostolic Church.
I confess one Baptism for the forgiveness of sins
and I look forward to the resurrection of the dead
and the life of the world to come. Amen.

The Apostles' Creed

Credo in Deum, Patrem omnipoténtem,
Creatórem cæli et terræ,
et in Iesum Christum, Fílium eius únicum,
Dóminum nostrum, *(all bow)*
qui concéptus est de Spíritu Sancto,
natus ex María Vírgine,
passus sub Póntio Piláto,
crucifíxus, mórtuus, et sepúltus,
descéndit ad ínferos,
tértia die resurréxit a mórtuis,
ascéndit ad cælos,
sedet ad déxteram Dei Patris omnipoténtis,
inde ventúrus est iudicáre vivos et mórtuos.

Credo in Spíritum Sanctum,
sanctam Ecclésiam cathólicam,
Sanctórum communiónem,
remissiónem peccatórum,
carnis resurrectiónem,
vitam ætérnam. Amen.

The Apostles' Creed

I believe in God,
the Father almighty
Creator of heaven and earth,
and in Jesus Christ, his only Son, our Lord, *(all bow)*
who was conceived by the Holy Spirit,
born of the Virgin Mary,
suffered under Pontius Pilate,
was crucified, died and was buried;
he descended into hell;
on the third day he rose again from the dead;
he ascended into heaven,
and is seated at the right hand of God
the Father almighty;
from there he will come to judge the living and the dead.

I believe in the Holy Spirit,
the holy catholic Church,
the communion of saints,
the forgiveness of sins,
the resurrection of the body,
and life everlasting. Amen.

The Prayer of the Faithful (Bidding Prayers)

Intentions will normally be for the Church; for the world; for those in particular need; and for the local community. After each there is time for silent prayer, followed by the next intention, or concluded with a sung phrase such as Christe audi nos, *or* Christe exaudi nos, *or by a responsory such as:*

R. **Præsta, ætérne omnípotens Deus.** *Or:*
R. **Te rogámus audi nos.** *Or:*
R. **Kýrie, eléison.**

The Priest concludes the Prayer with a collect.

The Prayer of the Faithful (Bidding Prayers)

Intentions will normally be for the Church; for the world; for those in particular need; and for the local community. After each there is time for silent prayer, followed by the next intention, or concluded with a sung phrase such as Christ, hear us, *or* Christ graciously hear us, *or by a responsory such as*:

Let us pray to the Lord.
R. Grant this, almighty God. *Or*:
R. Lord, have mercy. *Or*:
R. Kýrie, eléison.

The Priest concludes the Prayer with a collect.

The Liturgy of the Eucharist

For Catholics, the Eucharist is the source and summit of the whole Christian life.

After the Liturgy of the Word, the people sit and the Offertory Chant begins. The faithful express their participation by making an offering, bringing forward bread and wine for the celebration of the Eucharist.

Preparatory Prayers

Standing at the altar, the Priest takes the paten with the bread and holds it slightly raised above the altar with both hands, saying:

Pr. Benedíctus es, Dómine, Deus univérsi,
quia de tua largitáte accépimus panem,
quem tibi offérimus,
fructum terræ et óperis mánuum hóminum:
ex quo nobis fiet panis vitæ.

R. Benedíctus Deus in sǽcula.

The Priest then takes the chalice and holds it slightly raised above the altar with both hands, saying:

Pr. Benedíctus es, Dómine, Deus univérsi,
quia de tua largitáte accépimus vinum,
quod tibi offérimus,
fructum vitis et óperis mánuum hóminum,
ex quo nobis fiet potus spiritális.

R. Benedíctus Deus in sǽcula.

The Liturgy of the Eucharist

For Catholics, the Eucharist is the source and summit of the whole Christian life.

After the Liturgy of the Word, the people sit and the Offertory Chant begins. The faithful express their participation by making an offering, bringing forward bread and wine for the celebration of the Eucharist.

Preparatory Prayers

Standing at the altar, the Priest takes the paten with the bread and holds it slightly raised above the altar with both hands, saying:

Pr. Blessed are you, Lord God of all creation,
for through your goodness we have received
the bread we offer you:
fruit of the earth and work of human hands,
it will become for us the bread of life.

R. Blessed be God for ever.

The Priest then takes the chalice and holds it slightly raised above the altar with both hands, saying:

Pr. Blessed are you, Lord God of all creation,
for through your goodness we have received
the wine we offer you:
fruit of the vine and work of human hands,
it will become our spiritual drink.

R. Blessed be God for ever.

The Priest completes additional personal preparatory rites, and the people rise as he says:

Pr. Oráte, fratres:
ut meum ac vestrum sacrifícium
acceptábile fiat apud Deum Patrem omnipoténtem.

**R. Suscípiat Dóminus sacrifícium de mánibus tuis
ad laudem et glóriam nóminis sui,
ad utilitátem quoque nostram
totiúsque Ecclésiæ suæ sanctæ.**

The Prayer over the Offerings

The Priest says the Prayer over the Offerings, at the end of which the people acclaim:

R. Amen.

The Priest completes additional personal preparatory rites, and the people rise as he says:

Pr. Pray, brethren (brothers and sisters),
that my sacrifice and yours
may be acceptable to God,
the almighty Father.

R. May the Lord accept the sacrifice at your hands
for the praise and glory of his name,
for our good
and the good of all his holy Church.

The Prayer over the Offerings

The Priest says the Prayer over the Offerings, at the end of which the people acclaim:

R. Amen.

The Eucharistic Prayer

Extending his hands, the Priest says:

Pr. Dóminus vobíscum.

R. Et cum spíritu tuo.

Pr. Sursum corda.

R. Habémus ad Dóminum.

Pr. Grátias agámus Dómino Deo nostro.

R. Dignum et iustum est.

The Priest continues with the Preface appropriate to the Season or Feast at the end of which all sing or say:

Sanctus, Sanctus, Sanctus, Dóminus Deus Sábaoth.
Pleni sunt cæli et terra glória tua.
Hosánna in excélsis.
Benedíctus qui venit in nómine Dómini.
Hosánna in excélsis.

After the Sanctus the congregation kneels for the remainder of the Eucharistic Prayer. (Texts for the four principal Eucharistic Prayers follow: Eucharistic Prayer I at p. 30, *II at p.* 44, *III at p.* 56, *IV at p.* 68.*)*

The Eucharistic Prayer

Extending his hands, the Priest says:

Pr. The Lord be with you.

R. And with your spirit.

Pr. Lift up your hearts.

R. We lift them up to the Lord.

Pr. Let us give thanks to the Lord our God.

R. It is right and just.

The Priest continues with the Preface appropriate to the Season or Feast at the end of which all sing or say:

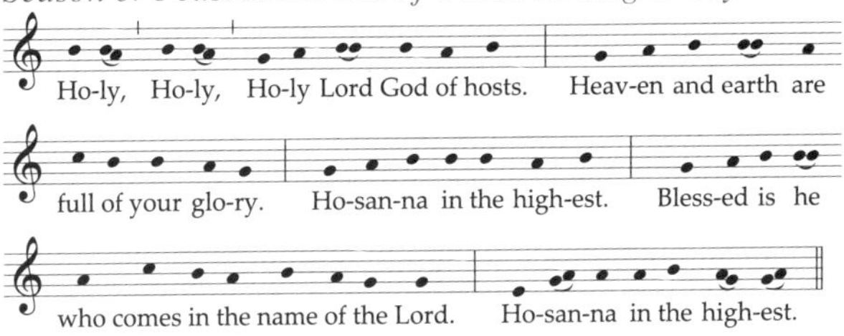

Holy, Holy, Holy Lord God of hosts.
Heaven and earth are full of your glory.
Hosanna in the highest.
Blessed is he who comes in the name of the Lord.
Hosanna in the highest.

After the Sanctus the congregation kneels for the remainder of the Eucharistic Prayer. (Texts for the four principal Eucharistic Prayers follow: Eucharistic Prayer I at p. 31, *II at p.* 45, *III at p.* 57, *IV at p.* 69.)

Eucharistic Prayer I
(The Roman Canon)

Te ígitur, clementíssime Pater, per Iesum Christum,
Fílium tuum,
Dóminum nostrum,
súpplices rogámus ac pétimus,
uti accépta hábeas
et benedícas ✠ hæc dona, hæc múnera,
hæc sancta sacrifícia illibáta,
in primis, quæ tibi offérimus
pro Ecclésia tua sancta cathólica:
quam pacificáre, custodíre, adunáre
et régere dignéris toto orbe terrárum:
una cum fámulo tuo Papa nostro N.
et Antístite nostro N*.
et ómnibus orthodóxis atque cathólicæ
et apostólicæ fídei cultóribus.

Commemoration of the Living.

Meménto, Dómine,
famulórum famularúmque tuárum N. et N.
et ómnium circumstántium,
quorum tibi fides cógnita est et nota devótio,
pro quibus tibi offérimus:
vel qui tibi ófferunt hoc sacrifícium laudis,
pro se suísque ómnibus:
pro redemptióne animarúm suárum,
pre spe salútis et incolumitátis suæ:

---

* Mention may be made here of the Coadjutor Bishop, or Auxiliary Bishops.

Eucharistic Prayer I
(The Roman Canon)

Pr. To you, therefore, most merciful Father,
we make humble prayer and petition
through Jesus Christ, your Son, our Lord:
that you accept
and bless ✠ these gifts, these offerings,
these holy and unblemished sacrifices,
which we offer you firstly
for your holy catholic Church.
Be pleased to grant her peace,
to guard, unite and govern her
throughout the whole world,
together with your servant N. our Pope
and N. our Bishop,*
and all those who, holding to the truth,
hand on the catholic and apostolic faith.

Commemoration of the Living.
Remember, Lord, your servants N. and N.
and all gathered here,
whose faith and devotion are known to you.
For them, we offer you this sacrifice of praise
or they offer it for themselves
and all who are dear to them:
for the redemption of their souls,
in hope of health and well-being,

* Mention may be made here of the Coadjutor Bishop, or Auxiliary Bishops.

tibíque reddunt vota sua
ætérno Deo, vivo et vero.

Within the Action.

Communicántes,
et memóriam venerántes,
in primis gloriósæ semper Vírginis Maríæ,
Genetrícis Dei et Dómini nostri Iesu Christi:
sed et béati Ioseph, eiúsdem Vírginis Sponsi,
et beatórum Apostolórum ac Mártyrum tuórum,
Petri et Pauli, Andréæ,
(Iacóbi, Ioánnis,
Thomæ, Iacóbi, Philíppi,
Bartholomǽi, Matthǽi,
Simónis et Thaddǽi:
Lini, Cleti, Cleméntis, Xysti,
Cornélii, Cypriáni,
Lauréntii, Chrysógoni,
Ioánnis et Pauli,
Cosmæ et Damiáni)
et ómnium Sanctórum tuórum;
quorum méritis precibúsque concédas,
ut in ómnibus protectiónis tuæ muniámur auxílio.
(Per Christum Dóminum nostrum. Amen.)

Hanc ígitur oblatiónem servitútis nostræ,
sed et cunctæ famíliæ tuæ,
quǽsumus, Dómine, ut placátus accípias:

and paying their homage to you,
the eternal God, living and true.

Within the Action.

In communion with those whose memory we venerate,
especially the glorious ever-Virgin Mary,
Mother of our God and Lord, Jesus Christ,
and blessed Joseph, her Spouse,
your blessed Apostles and Martyrs,
Peter and Paul, Andrew,
(James, John,
Thomas, James, Philip,
Bartholomew, Matthew,
Simon and Jude;
Linus, Cletus, Clement, Sixtus,
Cornelius, Cyprian,
Lawrence, Chrysogonus,
John and Paul,
Cosmas and Damian)
and all your Saints;
we ask that through their merits and prayers,
in all things we may be defended
by your protecting help.
(Through Christ our Lord. Amen.)

Therefore, Lord, we pray:
graciously accept this oblation of our service,
that of your whole family;

diésque nostros in tua pace dispónas,
atque ab ætérna damnatióne nos éripi
et in electórum tuórum iúbeas grege numerári.
(Per Christum Dóminum nostrum. Amen.)

Quam oblatiónem tu, Deus, in ómnibus, quǽsumus,
benedíctam, adscríptam, ratam,
rationábilem, acceptabilémque fácere dignéris:
ut nobis Corpus et Sanguis fiat dilectíssimi Fílii tui,
Dómini nostri Iesu Christi.
Qui, prídie quam paterétur,
accépit panem in sanctas ac venerábiles manus suas,
et elevátis óculis in cælum
ad te Deum Patrem suum omnipoténtem,
tibi grátias agens benedíxit,
fregit,
dedítque discípulis suis, dicens:

ACCÍPITE ET MANDUCÁTE EX HOC OMNES:
HOC EST ENIM CORPUS MEUM,
QUOD PRO VOBIS TRADÉTUR.

Símili modo, postquam cenátum est,
accípiens et hunc præclárum cálicem
in sanctas ac venerábiles manus suas,
item tibi grátias agens benedíxit,
dedítque discípulis suis dicens:

order our days in your peace,
and command that we be delivered from eternal damnation
and counted among the flock of those you have chosen.
(Through Christ Our Lord. Amen.)

Be pleased, O God, we pray,
to bless, acknowledge,
and approve this offering in every respect;
make it spiritual and acceptable,
so that it may become for us
the Body and Blood of your most beloved Son,
our Lord Jesus Christ.
On the day before he was to suffer,
he took bread in his holy and venerable hands,
and with eyes raised to heaven
to you, O God, his almighty Father,
giving you thanks, he said the blessing,
broke the bread
and gave it to his disciples, saying:

> 'TAKE THIS, ALL OF YOU, AND EAT OF IT,
> FOR THIS IS MY BODY,
> WHICH WILL BE GIVEN UP FOR YOU.'

In a similar way, when supper was ended,
he took this precious chalice
in his holy and venerable hands,
and once more giving you thanks, he said the blessing
and gave the chalice to his disciples, saying:

ACCÍPITE ET BÍBITE EX EO OMNES:
HIC EST ENIM CALIX SÁNGUINIS MEI
NOVI ET ÆTÉRNI TESTAMÉNTI,
QUI PRO VOBIS ET PRO MULTIS EFFUNDÉTUR
IN REMISSIÓNEM PECCATÓRUM.

HOC FÁCITE IN MEAM COMMEMORATIÓNEM.

Pr. Mystérium fídei.

The people continue, acclaiming one of the following:

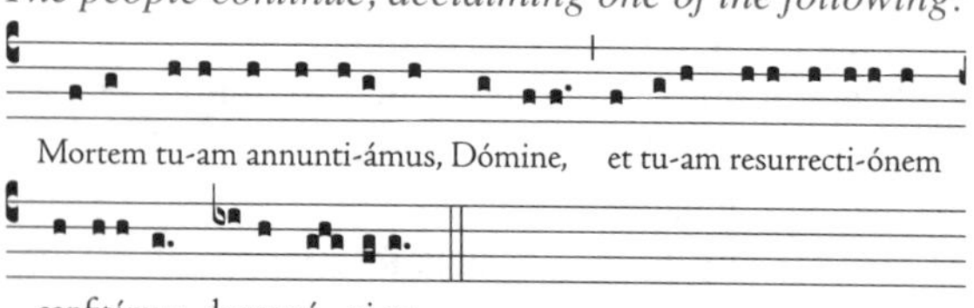

**1. Mortem tuam annuntiámus, Dómine,
et tuam resurrectiónem confitémur, donec vénias.**

**2. Quotiescúmque manducámus panem hunc
et cálicem bíbimus,
mortem tuam annuntiámus, Dómine, donec vénias.**

'TAKE THIS, ALL OF YOU, AND DRINK FROM IT,
FOR THIS IS THE CHALICE OF MY BLOOD,
THE BLOOD OF THE NEW AND ETERNAL COVENANT,
WHICH WILL BE POURED OUT FOR YOU AND FOR MANY
FOR THE FORGIVENESS OF SINS.

DO THIS IN MEMORY OF ME.'

Pr. The mystery of faith.

The people continue, acclaiming one of the following:

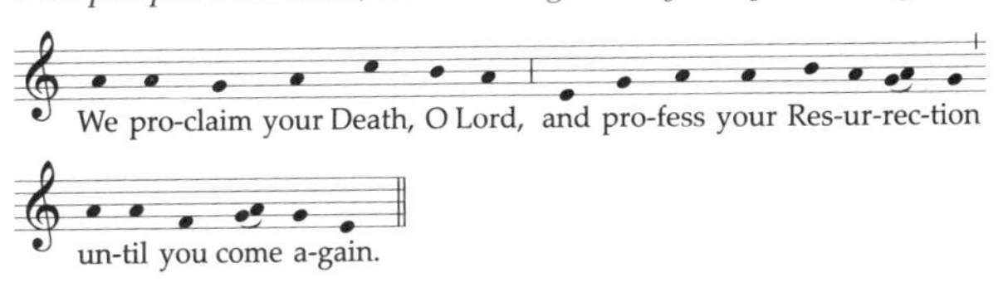

**1. We proclaim your Death, O Lord,
and profess your Resurrection
until you come again.**

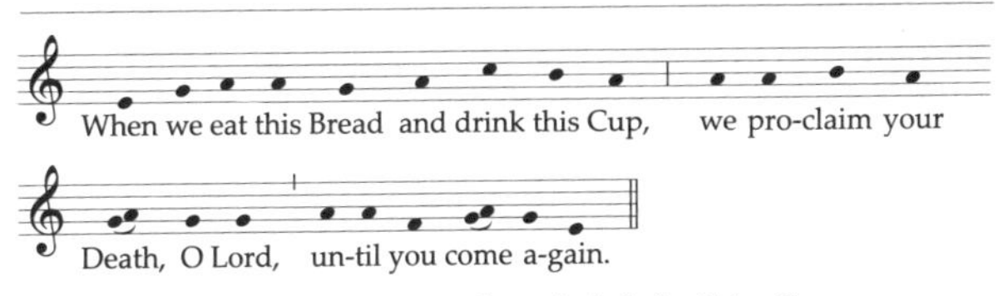

**2. When we eat this Bread and drink this Cup,
we proclaim your Death, O Lord,
until you come again.**

3. Salvátor mundi, salva nos,
qui per crucem et resurrectiónem tuam liberásti nos.

Pr. Unde et mémores, Dómine,
nos servi tui,
sed et plebs tua sancta,
eiúsdem Christi, Fílii tui, Dómini nostri,
tam beátæ passiónis,
necnon et ab ínferis resurrectiónis,
sed et in cælos gloriósæ ascensiónis:
offérimus præcláræ maiestáti tuæ
de tuis donis ac datis
hóstiam puram,
hóstiam sanctam,
hóstiam immaculátam,
Panem sanctum vitæ ætérnæ
et Cálicem salútis perpétuæ.

Supra quæ propítio ac seréno vultu
respícere dignéris:
et accépta habére,
sícuti accépta habére dignátus es

3. Save us, Saviour of the world,
for by your Cross and Resurrection
you have set us free.

Pr. Therefore, O Lord,
as we celebrate the memorial of the blessed Passion,
the Resurrection from the dead,
and the glorious Ascension into heaven
of Christ, your Son, our Lord,
we, your servants and your holy people,
offer to your glorious majesty
from the gifts that you have given us,
this pure victim,
this holy victim,
this spotless victim,
the holy Bread of eternal life
and the Chalice of everlasting salvation.

Be pleased to look upon these offerings
with a serene and kindly countenance,
and to accept them,
as once you were pleased to accept

múnera púeri tui iusti Abel,
et sacrifícium Patriárchæ nostri Abrahæ,
et quod tibi óbtulit summus sacérdos tuus Melchísedech,
sanctum sacrifícium, immaculátam hóstiam.
Súpplices te rogámus, omnípotens Deus:
iube hæc perférri per manus sancti Angeli tui
in sublíme altáre tuum,
in conspéctu divínæ maiestátis tuæ;
ut, quotquot ex hac altáris participatióne
sacrosánctum Fílii tui Corpus et Sánguinem sumpsérimus,
omni benedictióne cælésti et grátia repleámur
(Per Christum Dóminum nostrum. Amen.)

Commemoration of the Dead

Meménto étiam, Dómine, famulórum famularúmque
tuárum N. et N.,
qui nos præcessérunt cum signo fídei,
et dórmiunt in somno pacis.
Ipsis, Dómine, et ómnibus in Christo quiescéntibus,
locum refrigérii, lucis et pacis,
ut indúlgeas, deprecámur.
(Per Christum Dóminum nostrum. Amen.)

Nobis quoque peccatóribus fámulis tuis,
de multitúdine miseratiónum tuárum sperántibus,
partem áliquam et societátem donáre dignéris
cum tuis sanctis Apóstolis et Martýribus:

the gifts of your servant Abel the just,
the sacrifice of Abraham, our father in faith,
and the offering of your high priest Melchizedek,
a holy sacrifice, a spotless victim.
In humble prayer we ask you, almighty God:
command that these gifts be borne
by the hands of your holy Angel
to your altar on high
in the sight of your divine majesty,
so that all of us, who through this participation at the altar
receive the most holy Body and Blood of your Son,
may be filled with every grace and heavenly blessing.
(Through Christ our Lord. Amen.)

Commemoration of the Dead

Remember also, Lord, your servants N. and N.,
who have gone before us with the sign of faith
and rest in the sleep of peace.
Grant them, O Lord, we pray,
and all who sleep in Christ,
a place of refreshment, light and peace.
(Through Christ our Lord. Amen.)

To us, also, your servants, who, though sinners,
hope in your abundant mercies,
graciously grant some share
and fellowship with your holy Apostles and Martyrs:

cum Ioánne, Stéphano,
Matthía, Bárnaba,
(Ignátio, Alexándro,
Marcellíno, Petro,
Felicitáte, Perpétua,
Agatha, Lúcia,
Agnéte, Cæcília, Anastásia)
et ómnibus Sanctis tuis:
intra quorum nos consórtium,
non æstimátor mériti,
sed véniæ, quǽsumus, largítor admítte.
Per Christum Dóminum nostrum.

Per quem hæc ómnia, Dómine,
semper bona creas, sanctíficas, vivíficas, benedícis,
et præstas nobis.

The Priest takes the chalice and the paten with the host:

Pr. Per ipsum, et cum ipso, et in ipso,
est tibi Deo Patri omnipoténti,
in unitáte Spíritus Sancti,
omnis honor et glória
per ómnia sǽcula sæculórum.
R. Amen.

Then follows the Communion Rite, p. 82.

---

with John the Baptist, Stephen,
Matthias, Barnabas,
(Ignatius, Alexander,
Marcellinus, Peter,
Felicity, Perpetua,
Agatha, Lucy,
Agnes, Cecilia, Anastasia)
and all your Saints;
admit us, we beseech you,
into their company,
not weighing our merits,
but granting us your pardon,
through Christ our Lord.

Through whom
you continue to make all these good things, O Lord;
you sanctify them, fill them with life,
bless them, and bestow them upon us.

The Priest takes the chalice and the paten with the host:

Pr. Through him, and with him, and in him,
O God, almighty Father,
in the unity of the Holy Spirit,
all glory and honour is yours,
for ever and ever.

R. Amen.

Then follows the Communion Rite, p. 83.

Eucharistic Prayer II

Pr. Dóminus vóbiscum.
R. Et cum spíritu tuo.
Pr. Sursum corda.
R. Habémus ad Dóminum.
Pr. Grátias agámus Dómino Deo nostro.
R. Dignum et iustum est.

Pr. Vere dignum et iustum est, æquum et salutáre, nos tibi, sancte Pater,
semper et ubíque grátias ágere
per Fílium dilectiónis tuæ Iesum Christum,
Verbum tuum per quod cuncta fecísti:
quem misísti nobis Salvatórem et Redemptórem,
incarnátum de Spíritu Sancto et ex Vírgine natum.

Qui voluntátem tuam adímplens
et pópulum tibi sanctum acquírens
exténdit manus cum paterétur,
ut mortem sólveret et resurrectiónem manifestáret.

Et ídeo cum Angelis et ómnibus Sanctis
glóriam tuam prædicámus, una voce dicéntes:

Eucharistic Prayer II

Pr. The Lord be with you.
R. And with your spirit.
Pr. Lift up your hearts.
R. We lift them up to the Lord.
Pr. Let us give thanks to the Lord our God.
R. It is right and just.

Pr. It is truly right and just, our duty and our salvation,
always and everywhere to give you thanks, Father most holy,
through your beloved Son, Jesus Christ,
your Word through whom you made all things,
whom you sent as our Saviour and Redeemer,
incarnate by the Holy Spirit and born of the Virgin.

Fulfilling your will and gaining for you a holy people,
he stretched out his hands as he endured his Passion,
so as to break the bonds of death and manifest the resurrection.

And so, with the Angels and all the Saints
we declare your glory,
as with one voice we acclaim:

The people sing or say aloud the Sanctus.

Sanctus, Sanctus, Sanctus Dóminus Deus Sábaoth.
Pleni sunt cæli et terra glória tua.
Hosánna in excélsis.
Benedíctus qui venit in nómine Dómini.
Hosánna in excélsis.

Pr. Vere Sanctus es, Dómine, fons omnis sanctitátis.
Hæc ergo dona, quǽsumus,
Spíritus tui rore sanctífica,
ut nobis Corpus et ✠ Sanguis fiant
Dómini nostri Iesu Christi.

The people sing or say aloud the Sanctus.

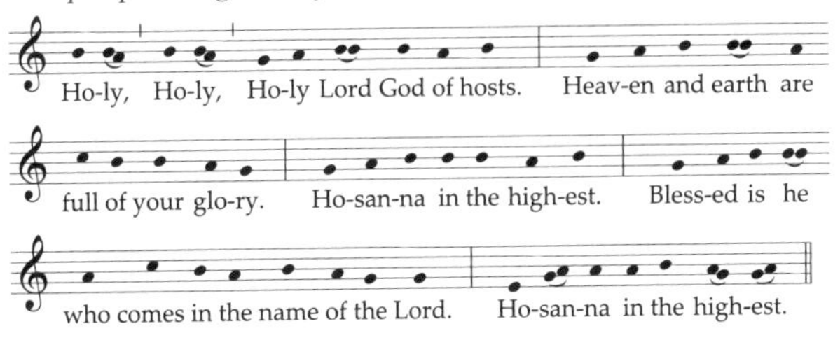

Holy, Holy, Holy Lord God of hosts.
Heaven and earth are full of your glory.
Hosanna in the highest.
Blessed is he who comes in the name of the Lord.
Hosanna in the highest.

Pr. You are indeed Holy, O Lord,
the fount of all holiness.
Make holy, therefore, these gifts, we pray,
by sending down your Spirit upon them like the dewfall,
so that they may become for us
the Body and ✠ Blood of our Lord Jesus Christ.

Qui cum Passióni voluntárie traderétur,
accépit panem et grátias agens fregit,
dedítque discípulis suis, dicens:

ACCÍPITE ET MANDUCÁTE EX HOC OMNES:
HOC EST ENIM CORPUS MEUM,
QUOD PRO VOBIS TRADÉTUR.

Símili modo, postquam cenátum est,
accípiens et cálicem,
íterum grátias agens dedit discípulis suis, dicens:

ACCÍPITE ET BÍBITE EX EO OMNES:
HIC EST ENIM CALIX SÁNGUINIS MEI
NOVI ET ÆTÉRNI TESTAMÉNTI,
QUI PRO VOBIS ET PRO MULTIS EFFUNDÉTUR
IN REMISSIÓNEM PECCATÓRUM.

HOC FÁCITE IN MEAM COMMEMORATIÓNEM.

Pr. Mystérium fídei.

At the time he was betrayed
and entered willingly into his Passion,
he took bread and, giving thanks, broke it,
and gave it to his disciples, saying:

'TAKE THIS, ALL OF YOU, AND EAT OF IT,
FOR THIS IS MY BODY,
WHICH WILL BE GIVEN UP FOR YOU.'

In a similar way, when supper was ended,
he took the chalice
and, once more giving thanks,
he gave it to his disciples, saying:

'TAKE THIS, ALL OF YOU, AND DRINK FROM IT,
FOR THIS IS THE CHALICE OF MY BLOOD,
THE BLOOD OF THE NEW AND ETERNAL COVENANT,
WHICH WILL BE POURED OUT FOR YOU AND FOR MANY
FOR THE FORGIVENESS OF SINS.

DO THIS IN MEMORY OF ME.'

Pr. The mystery of faith.

The people continue, acclaiming one of the following:

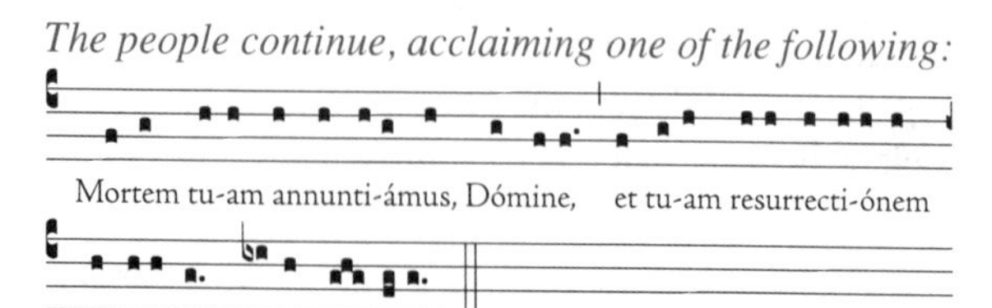

1. Mortem tuam annuntiámus, Dómine,
et tuam resurrectiónem confitémur, donec vénias.

2. Quotiescúmque manducámus panem hunc
et cálicem bíbimus,
mortem tuam annuntiámus, Dómine, donec vénias.

Salvátor mundi, salva nos, qui per crucem et resurrecti-ónem tu-am
li-be-rá- sti nos.

3. Salvátor mundi, salva nos,
qui per crucem et resurrectiónem tuam liberásti nos.

The people continue, acclaiming one of the following:

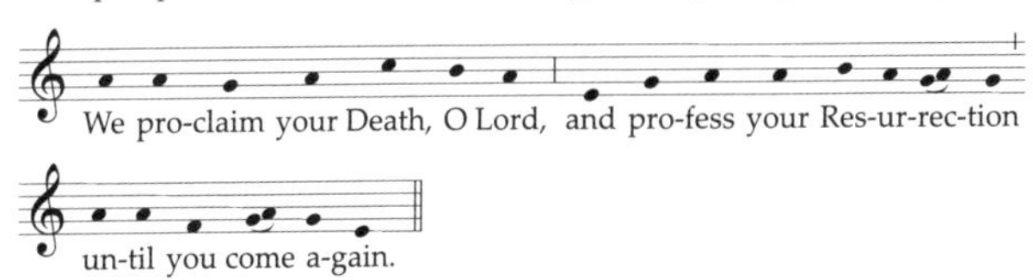

1. We proclaim your Death, O Lord,
and profess your Resurrection
until you come again.

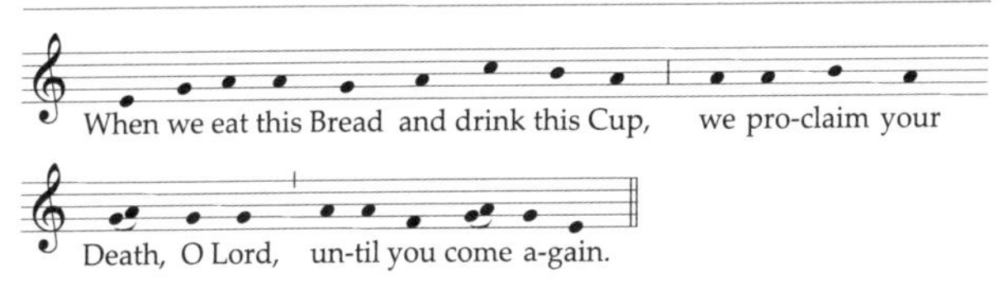

2. When we eat this Bread and drink this Cup,
we proclaim your Death, O Lord,
until you come again.

3. Save us, Saviour of the world,
for by your Cross and Resurrection
you have set us free.

Pr. Mémores ígitur mortis et resurrectiónis eius,
tibi, Dómine, panem vitæ
et cálicem salútis offérimus,
grátias agéntes quia nos dignos habuísti
astáre coram te et tibi ministráre.

Et súpplices deprecámur
ut Córporis et Sánguinis Christi partícipes
a Spíritu Sancto congregémur in unum.
Recordáre, Dómine, Ecclésiæ tuæ toto orbe diffúsæ,
ut eam in caritáte perfícias
una cum Papa nostro N. et Epíscopo nostro N.*
et univérso clero.

In Masses for the Dead, the following may be added:
Meménto fámuli tui (fámulæ tuæ) N.,
quem (quam) (hódie) ad te ex hoc mundo vocásti.
Concéde, ut, qui (quæ) complantátus (complantáta) fuit
similitúdini mortis Fílii tui,
simul fiat et resurrectiónis ipsíus.

Meménto étiam fratrum nostrórum,
qui in spe resurrectiónis dormiérunt,
omniúmque in tua miseratióne defunctórum,
et eos in lumen vultus tui admítte.

* Mention may be made here of the Coadjutor Bishop, or Auxiliary Bishops.

Pr. Therefore, as we celebrate
the memorial of his Death and Resurrection,
we offer you, Lord,
the Bread of life and the Chalice of salvation,
giving thanks that you have held us worthy
to be in your presence and minister to you.
Humbly we pray
that, partaking of the Body and Blood of Christ,
we may be gathered into one by the Holy Spirit.
Remember, Lord, your Church,
spread throughout the world,
and bring her to the fullness of charity,
together with N. our Pope and N. our Bishop*
and all the clergy.

In Masses for the Dead, the following may be added:

Remember your servant N.,
whom you have called (today)
from this world to yourself.
Grant that he (she) who was united with your Son
in a death like his,
may also be one with him in his Resurrection.

Remember also our brothers and sisters
who have fallen asleep in the hope of the resurrection,
and all who have died in your mercy:
welcome them into the light of your face.

---

* Mention may be made here of the Coadjutor Bishop, or Auxiliary Bishops.

Omnium nostrum, quǽsumus, miserére,
ut cum beáta Dei Genetríce Vírgine María,
beátis Apostólis et ómnibus Sanctis,
qui tibi a sǽculo placuérunt,
ætérnæ vitæ mereámur esse consórtes,
et te laudémus et glorificémus
per Fílium tuum Iesum Christum.

The Priest takes the chalice and the paten with the host:

Per ipsum, et cum ipso, et in ipso,
est tibi Deo Patri omnipoténti,
in unitáte Spíritus Sancti,
omnis honor et glória
per ómnia sǽcula sæculórum.

R. Amen.

Then follows the Communion Rite, p. 82.

Have mercy on us all, we pray,
that with the Blessed Virgin Mary, Mother of God,
with the blessed Apostles,
and all the Saints who have pleased you throughout the ages,
we may merit to be coheirs to eternal life,
and may praise and glorify you
through your Son, Jesus Christ.

The Priest takes the chalice and the paten with the host:
Through him, and with him, and in him,
O God, almighty Father,
in the unity of the Holy Spirit,
all glory and honour is yours,
for ever and ever.
R. Amen.

Then follows the Communion Rite, p. 83.

Eucharistic Prayer III

Pr. Vere Sanctus es, Dómine,
et mérito te laudat omnis a te cóndita creatúra,
quia per Fílium tuum,
Dóminum nostrum Iesum Christum,
Spíritus Sancti operánte virtúte,
vivíficas et sanctíficas univérsa,
et pópulum tibi congregáre non désinis,
ut a solis ortu usque ad occásum
oblátio munda offerátur nómini tuo.

Súpplices ergo te, Dómine, deprecámur,
ut hæc múnera, quæ tibi sacránda detúlimus,
eódem Spíritu sanctificáre dignéris,
ut Corpus et ✠ Sanguis fiant
Fílii tui Dómini nostri Iesu Christi,
cuius mandáto hæc mystéria celebrámus.

Ipse enim in qua nocte tradebátur
accépit panem
et tibi grátias agens benedíxit,
fregit, dedítque discípulis suis, dicens:

ACCÍPITE ET MANDUCÁTE EX HOC OMNES:
HOC EST ENIM CORPUS MEUM,
QUOD PRO VOBIS TRADÉTUR.

Símili modo, postquam cenátum est,
accípiens cálicem,

Eucharistic Prayer III

Pr. You are indeed Holy, O Lord,
and all you have created
rightly gives you praise,
for through your Son our Lord Jesus Christ,
by the power and working of the Holy Spirit,
you give life to all things and make them holy,
and you never cease to gather a people to yourself,
so that from the rising of the sun to its setting
a pure sacrifice may be offered to your name.

Therefore, O Lord, we humbly implore you:
by the same Spirit graciously make holy
these gifts we have brought to you for consecration,
that they may become the Body and ✠ Blood
of your Son our Lord Jesus Christ,
at whose command we celebrate these mysteries.

For on the night he was betrayed
he himself took bread,
and, giving you thanks, he said the blessing,
broke the bread and gave it to his disciples, saying:

'TAKE THIS, ALL OF YOU, AND EAT OF IT,
FOR THIS IS MY BODY,
WHICH WILL BE GIVEN UP FOR YOU.'

In a similar way, when supper was ended,
he took the chalice,

et tibi grátias agens benedíxit,
dedítque discípulis suis, dicens:

ACCÍPITE ET BÍBITE EX EO OMNES:
HIC EST ENIM CALIX SÁNGUINIS MEI
NOVI ET ÆTÉRNI TESTAMÉNTI,
QUI PRO VOBIS ET PRO MULTIS EFFUNDÉTUR
IN REMISSIÓNEM PECCATÓRUM.

HOC FÁCITE IN MEAM COMMEMORATIÓNEM.

Pr. Mystérium fídei.

The people continue, acclaiming one of the following:

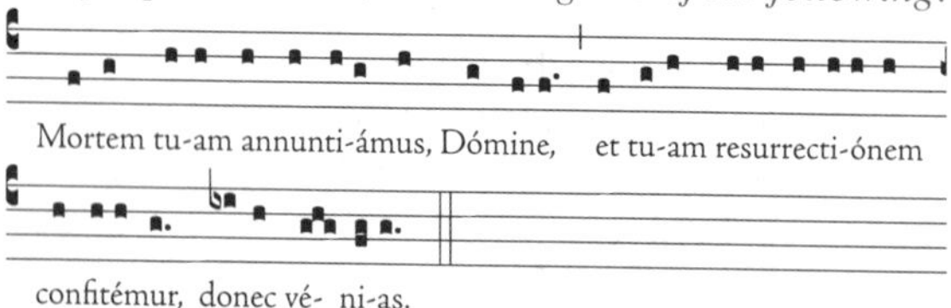

**1. Mortem tuam annuntiámus, Dómine,
et tuam resurrectiónem confitémur, donec vénias.**

**2. Quotiescúmque manducámus panem hunc
et cálicem bíbimus,
mortem tuam annuntiámus, Dómine, donec vénias.**

and, giving you thanks, he said the blessing,
and gave the chalice to his disciples, saying:

'TAKE THIS, ALL OF YOU, AND DRINK FROM IT,
FOR THIS IS THE CHALICE OF MY BLOOD,
THE BLOOD OF THE NEW AND ETERNAL COVENANT,
WHICH WILL BE POURED OUT FOR YOU AND FOR MANY
FOR THE FORGIVENESS OF SINS.

DO THIS IN MEMORY OF ME.'

Pr. The mystery of faith.

The people continue, acclaiming one of the following:

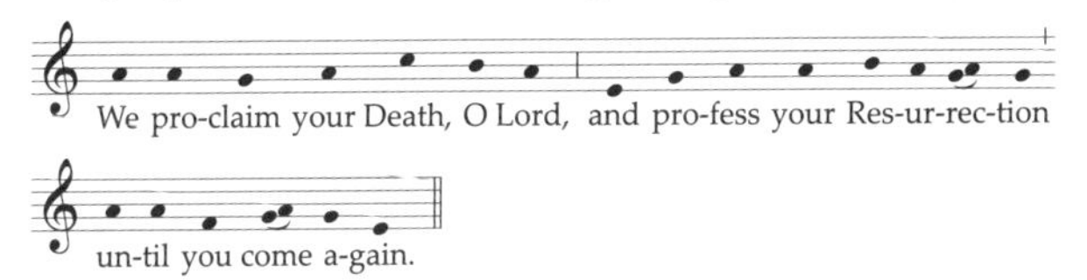

**1. We proclaim your Death, O Lord,
and profess your Resurrection
until you come again.**

**2. When we eat this Bread and drink this Cup,
we proclaim your Death, O Lord,
until you come again.**

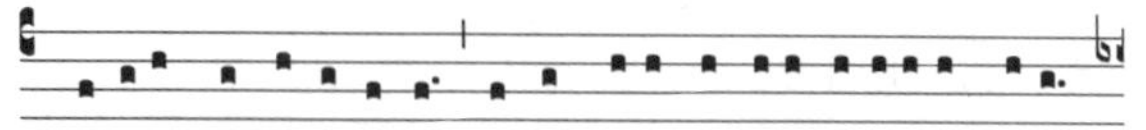

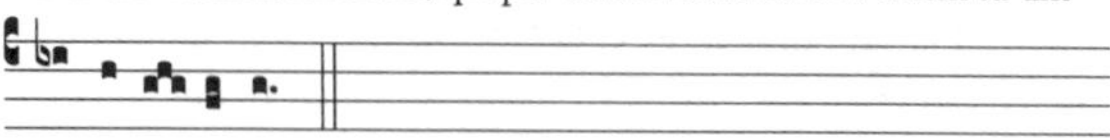

3. Salvátor mundi, salva nos,
qui per crucem et resurrectiónem tuam liberásti nos.

Pr. Mémores ígitur, Dómine,
eiúsdem Fílii tui salutíferæ passiónis
necnon mirábilis resurrectiónis
et ascensiónis in cælum,
sed et præstolántes álterum eius advéntum,
offérimus tibi, grátias referéntes,
hoc sacrifícium vivum et sanctum.

Réspice, quǽsumus, in oblatiónem Ecclésiæ tuæ
et, agnóscens Hóstiam,
cuius volúisti immolatióne placári,
concéde, ut qui Córpore et Sánguine Fílii tui refícimur,
Spíritu eius Sancto repléti,
unum corpus et unus spíritus inveniámur in Christo.

Ipse nos tibi perfíciat munus ætérnum,
ut cum eléctis tuis hereditátem cónsequi valeámus,

3. Save us, Saviour of the world,
for by your Cross and Resurrection
you have set us free.

Pr. Therefore, O Lord, as we celebrate the memorial
of the saving Passion of your Son,
his wondrous Resurrection
and Ascension into heaven,
and as we look forward to his second coming,
we offer you in thanksgiving
this holy and living sacrifice.

Look, we pray, upon the oblation of your Church
and, recognizing the sacrificial Victim by whose death
you willed to reconcile us to yourself,
grant that we, who are nourished
by the Body and Blood of your Son
and filled with his Holy Spirit,
may become one body, one spirit in Christ.

May he make of us
an eternal offering to you,
so that we may obtain an inheritance with your elect,

in primis cum beátissima Vírgine, Dei Genetríce, María,
cum beátis Apóstolis tuis et gloriósis Martýribus
(cum Sancto N.: *the saint of the day or Patron Saint*)
et ómnibus Sanctis,
quorum intercessióne
perpétuo apud te confídimus adiuvári.

Hæc Hóstia nostræ reconciliatiónis profíciat,
quǽsumus, Dómine,
ad totíus mundi pacem atque salútem.
Ecclésiam tuam, peregrinántem in terra,
in fide et caritáte firmáre dignéris
cum fámulo tuo Papa nostro N. et Epíscopo nostro N.*,
cum episcopáli órdine et univérso clero
et omni pópulo acquisitiónis tuæ.
Votis huius famíliæ, quam tibi astáre voluísti,
adésto propítius.
Omnes fílios tuos ubíque dispérsos
tibi, clemens Pater, miserátus coniúnge.

Fratres nostros defúnctos
et omnes qui, tibi placéntes, ex hoc sǽculo transiérunt,
in regnum tuum benígnus admítte,
ubi fore sperámus,
ut simul glória tua perénniter satiémur,

* Mention may be made here of the Coadjutor Bishop, or Auxiliary Bishops.

especially with the most Blessed Virgin Mary,
  Mother of God,
with your blessed Apostles and glorious Martyrs
(with Saint N.: *the Saint of the day or Patron Saint*)
and with all the Saints,
on whose constant intercession in your presence
we rely for unfailing help.

May this Sacrifice of our reconciliation,
we pray, O Lord,
advance the peace and salvation of all the world.
Be pleased to confirm in faith and charity
your pilgrim Church on earth,
with your servant N. our Pope and N. our Bishop*,
the Order of Bishops, all the clergy,
and the entire people you have gained for your own.
Listen graciously to the prayers of this family,
whom you have summoned before you:
in your compassion, O merciful Father,
gather to yourself all your children
scattered throughout the world.

† To our departed brothers and sisters
and to all who were pleasing to you
at their passing from this life,
give kind admittance to your kingdom.

---

* Mention may be made here of the Coadjutor Bishop, or Auxiliary Bishops.

per Christum Dóminum nostrum,
per quem mundo bona cuncta largíris.

The Priest takes the chalice and the paten with the host:

Per ipsum, et cum ipso, et in ipso,
est tibi Deo Patri omnipoténti,
in unitáte Spíritus Sancti,
omnis honor et glória
per ómnia sǽcula sæculórum.
R. Amen.

Then follows the Communion Rite, p. 82.

When this Eucharistic Prayer is used in Masses for the Dead, the following may be said:

Meménto fámuli tui (fámulæ tuæ) N.,
quem (quam) (hódie) ad te ex hoc mundo vocásti.
Concéde, ut, qui (quæ) complantátus (complantáta)
fuit símilitudini mortis Fílii tui,
simul fiat et resurrectiónis ipsíus,
quando mórtuos suscitábit in carne de terra
et corpus humilitátis nostræ
configurábit córpori claritátis suæ.

There we hope to enjoy for ever the fullness of your glory
through Christ our Lord,
through whom you bestow on the world all that is good. †

The Priest takes the chalice and the paten with the host:

Through him, and with him, and in him,
O God, almighty Father,
in the unity of the Holy Spirit,
all glory and honour is yours,
for ever and ever.

R. Amen.

Then follows the Communion Rite, p. 83.

When this Eucharistic Prayer is used in Masses for the Dead, the following may be said:

† Remember your servant N.
whom you have called (today)
from this world to yourself.
Grant that he (she) who was united with your Son
in a death like his,
may also be one with him in his Resurrection,
when from the earth
he will raise up in the flesh those who have died,
and transform our lowly body
after the pattern of his own glorious body.

Sed et fratres nostros defúnctos,
et omnes qui, tibi placéntes, ex hoc sǽculo transiérunt,
in regnum tuum benígnus admítte,
ubi fore sperámus,
ut simul glória tua perénniter satiémur,
quando omnem lácrimam abstérges ab óculis nostris,
quia te, sícuti es, Deum nostrum vidéntes,
tibi símiles érimus cuncta per sǽcula,
et te sine fine laudábimus,
(*He joins his hands.*)
per Christum Dóminum nostrum,
per quem mundo bona cuncta largíris. †

To our departed brothers and sisters, too,
and to all who were pleasing to you
at their passing from this life,
give kind admittance to your kingdom.
There we hope to enjoy for ever the fullness of your glory,
when you will wipe away every tear from our eyes.
For seeing you, our God, as you are,
we shall be like you for all the ages
and praise you without end,
(He joins his hands.)
through Christ our Lord,
through whom you bestow on the world all that is good. †

Eucharistic Prayer IV

Pr. Dóminus vóbiscum.
R. **Et cum spíritu tuo.**
Pr. Sursum corda.
R. **Habémus ad Dóminum.**
Pr. Grátias agámus Dómino Deo nostro.
R. **Dignum et iustum est.**

Pr. Vere dignum est tibi grátias ágere,
vere iustum est te glorificáre, Pater sancte,
quia unus es Deus vivus et verus,
qui es ante sǽcula et pérmanes in ætérnum,
inaccessíbilem lucem inhábitans;
sed et qui unus bonus atque fons vitæ cuncta fecísti,
ut creatúras tuas benedictiónibus adimpléres
multásque lætificáres tui lúminis claritáte.

Et ídeo coram te innúmeræ astant turbæ Angelórum,
qui die ac nocte sérviunt tibi
et, vultus tui glóriam contempltes,
te incessánter gloríficant.

Cum quibus et nos et, per nostram vocem,
omnis quæ sub cælo est creatúra
nomen tuum in exsultatióne confitémur, canéntes:

Eucharistic Prayer IV

Pr. The Lord be with you.
R. **And with your spirit.**
Pr. Lift up your hearts.
R. **We lift them up to the Lord.**
Pr. Let us give thanks to the Lord our God.
R. **It is right and just.**

Pr. It is truly right to give you thanks,
truly just to give you glory, Father most holy,
for you are the one God living and true,
existing before all ages and abiding for all eternity,
dwelling in unapproachable light;
yet you, who alone are good, the source of life,
have made all that is,
so that you might fill your creatures with blessings
and bring joy to many of them by the glory of your light.

And so, in your presence are countless hosts of Angels,
who serve you day and night
and, gazing upon the glory of your face,
glorify you without ceasing.

With them we, too, confess your name in exultation,
giving voice to every creature under heaven,
as we acclaim:

The people sing or say aloud the Sanctus.

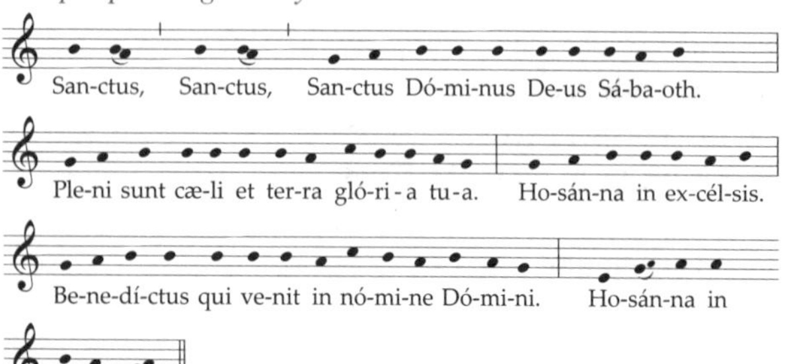

Sanctus, Sanctus, Sanctus Dóminus Deus Sábaoth.
Pleni sunt cæli et terra glória tua.
Hosánna in excélsis.
Benedíctus qui venit in nómine Dómini.
Hosánna in excélsis.

Pr. Confitémur tibi, Pater sancte,
quia magnus es et ómnia ópera tua
in sapiéntia et caritáte fecísti.
Hóminem ad tuam imáginem condidísti,
eíque commisísti mundi curam univérsi,
ut, tibi soli Creatóri sérviens,
creatúris ómnibus imperáret.
Et cum amicítiam tuam, non obœ́diens, amisísset,
non eum dereliquísti in mortis império.
Omnibus enim misericórditer subvenísti,
ut te quærentes invenírent.

The people sing or say aloud the Sanctus.

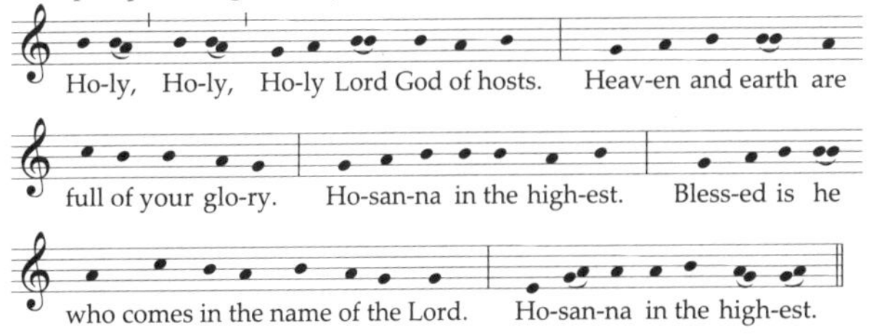

Holy, Holy, Holy Lord God of hosts.
Heaven and earth are full of your glory.
Hosanna in the highest.
Blessed is he who comes in the name of the Lord.
Hosanna in the highest.

Pr. We give you praise, Father most holy,
for you are great
and you have fashioned all your works
in wisdom and in love.
You formed man in your own image
and entrusted the whole world to his care,
so that in serving you alone, the Creator,
he might have dominion over all creatures.
And when through disobedience he had lost your friendship,
you did not abandon him to the domain of death.
For you came in mercy to the aid of all,
so that those who seek might find you.

Sed et fœdera plúries homínibus obtulísti
eósque per prophétas erudísti in exspectatióne salútis.

Et sic, Pater sancte, mundum dilexísti,
ut, compléta plenitúdine témporum,
Unigénitum tuum nobis mítteres Salvatórem.
Qui, incarnátus de Spíritu Sancto
et natus ex María Vírgine,
in nostra condiciónis forma est conversátus
per ómnia absque peccáto;
salútem evangelizávit paupéribus,
redemptiónem captívis,
mæstis corde lætítiam.
Ut tuam vero dispensatiónem impléret,
in mortem trádidit semetípsum
ac, resúrgens a mórtuis,
mortem destrúxit vitámque renovávit.

Et, ut non ámplius nobismetípsis viverémus,
sed sibi qui pro nobis mórtuus est atque surréxit,
a te, Pater, misit Spíritum Sanctum
primítias credéntibus,
qui, opus suum in mundo perfíciens,
omnem sanctificatiónem compléret.

Quǽsumus ígitur, Dómine,
ut idem Spíritus Sanctus
hæc múnera sanctificáre dignétur,

Time and again you offered them covenants
and through the prophets
taught them to look forward to salvation.

And you so loved the world, Father most holy,
that in the fullness of time
you sent your Only Begotten Son to be our Saviour.
Made incarnate by the Holy Spirit
and born of the Virgin Mary,
he shared our human nature
in all things but sin.
To the poor he proclaimed the good news of salvation,
to prisoners, freedom,
and to the sorrowful of heart, joy.
To accomplish your plan,
he gave himself up to death,
and, rising from the dead,
he destroyed death and restored life.

And that we might live no longer for ourselves
but for him who died and rose again for us,
he sent the Holy Spirit from you, Father,
as the first fruits for those who believe,
so that, bringing to perfection his work in the world,
he might sanctify creation to the full.

Therefore, O Lord, we pray:
may this same Holy Spirit
graciously sanctify these offerings,

ut Corpus et ✠ Sanguis fiant
Dómini nostri Iesu Christi
ad hoc magnum mystérium celebrándum,
quod ipse nobis relíquit in fœdus ætérnum.

Ipse enim, cum hora venísset
ut glorificarétur a te, Pater sancte,
ac dilexísset suos qui erant in mundo,
in finem diléxit eos:
et cenántibus illis
accépit panem, benedíxit ac fregit,
dedítque discípulis suis, dicens:

> ACCÍPITE ET MANDUCÁTE EX HOC OMNES:
> HOC EST ENIM CORPUS MEUM,
> QUOD PRO VOBIS TRADÉTUR.

Símili modo
accípiens cálicem, ex genímine vitis replétum,
grátias egit, dedítque discípulis suis, dicens:

> ACCÍPITE ET BÍBITE EX EO OMNES:
> HIC EST ENIM CALIX SÁNGUINIS MEI
> NOVI ET ÆTÉRNI TESTAMÉNTI,
> QUI PRO VOBIS ET PRO MULTIS EFFUNDÉTUR
> IN REMISSIÓNEM PECCATÓRUM.
>
> HOC FÁCITE IN MEAM COMMEMORATIÓNEM.

Pr. Mystérium fídei.

that they may become
the Body and ✠ Blood of our Lord Jesus Christ
for the celebration of this great mystery,
which he himself left us
as an eternal covenant.

For when the hour had come
for him to be glorified by you, Father most holy,
having loved his own who were in the world,
he loved them to the end:
and while they were at supper,
he took bread, blessed and broke it,
and gave it to his disciples, saying:

'TAKE THIS, ALL OF YOU, AND EAT OF IT,
FOR THIS IS MY BODY,
WHICH WILL BE GIVEN UP FOR YOU.'

In a similar way,
taking the chalice filled with the fruit of the vine,
he gave thanks,
and gave the chalice to his disciples, saying:

'TAKE THIS, ALL OF YOU, AND DRINK FROM IT,
FOR THIS IS THE CHALICE OF MY BLOOD,
THE BLOOD OF THE NEW AND ETERNAL COVENANT,
WHICH WILL BE POURED OUT FOR YOU AND FOR MANY
FOR THE FORGIVENESS OF SINS.

DO THIS IN MEMORY OF ME.'

Pr. The mystery of faith.

The people continue, acclaiming one of the following:

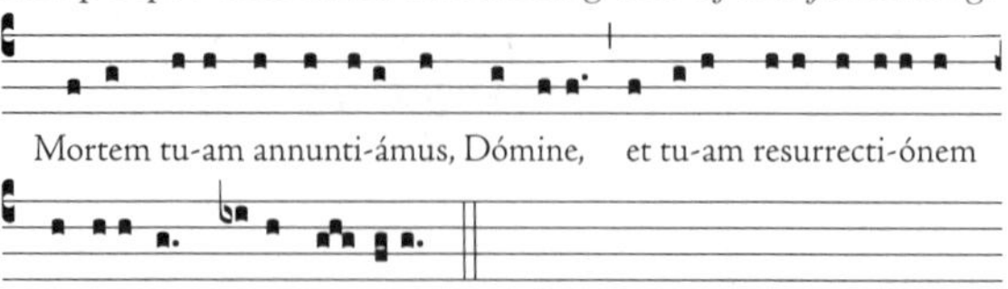

1. Mortem tuam annuntiámus, Dómine,
et tuam resurrectiónem confitémur, donec vénias.

2. Quotiescúmque manducámus panem hunc
et cálicem bíbimus,
mortem tuam annuntiámus, Dómine, donec vénias.

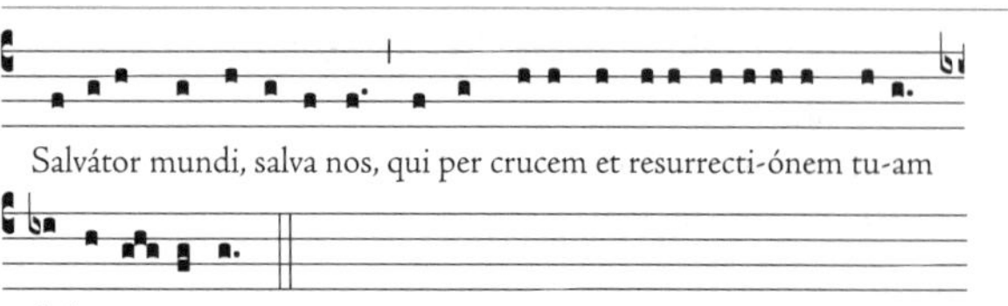

3. Salvátor mundi, salva nos,
qui per crucem et resurrectiónem tuam liberásti nos.

The people continue, acclaiming one of the following:

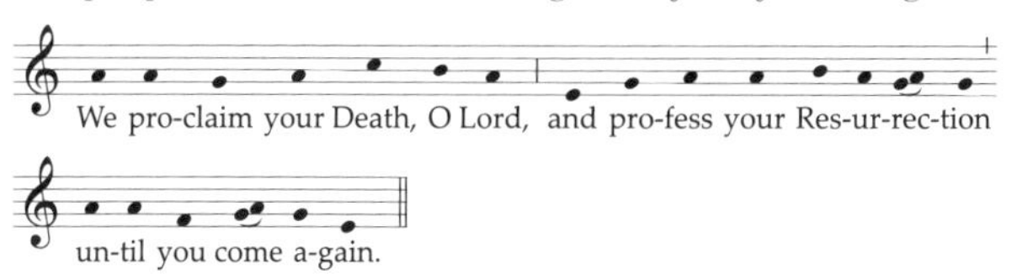

1. We proclaim your Death, O Lord,
and profess your Resurrection
until you come again.

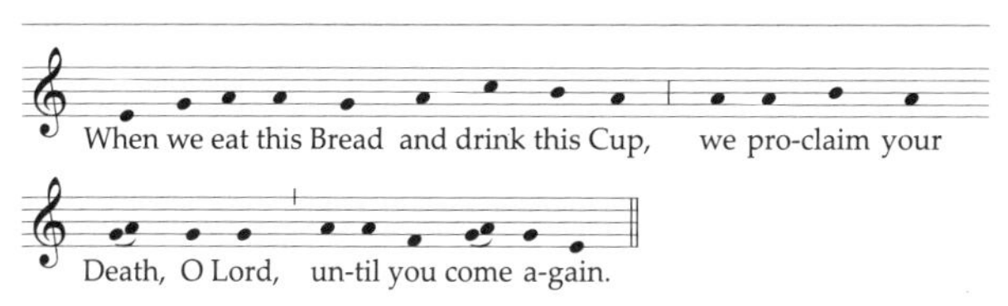

2. When we eat this Bread and drink this Cup,
we proclaim your Death, O Lord,
until you come again.

3. Save us, Saviour of the world,
for by your Cross and Resurrection
you have set us free.

Pr. Unde et nos, Dómine, redemptiónis nostræ memoriále nunc celebrántes,
mortem Christi
eiúsque descénsum ad ínferos recólimus,
eius resurrectiónem
et ascensiónem ad tuam déxteram profitémur,
et, exspectántes ipsíus advéntum in glória,
offérimus tibi eius Corpus et Sánguinem,
sacrifícium tibi acceptábile et toti mundo salutáre.

Réspice, Dómine, in Hóstiam,
quam Ecclésiæ tuæ ipse parásti,
et concéde benígnus ómnibus
qui ex hoc uno pane participábunt et cálice,
ut, in unum corpus a Sancto Spíritu congregáti,
in Christo hóstia viva perficiántur,
ad laudem glóriæ tuæ.
Nunc ergo, Dómine, ómnium recordáre,
pro quibus tibi hanc oblatiónem offérimus:
in primis fámuli tui, Papæ nostri N.,
Epíscopi nostri N.*, et Episcopórum órdinis univérsi,
sed et totíus cleri, et offeréntium,
et circumstántium,
et cuncti pópuli tui,
et ómnium, qui te quærunt corde sincéro.

---

* Mention may be made here of the Coadjutor Bishop, or Auxiliary Bishops.

Pr. Therefore, O Lord,
as we now celebrate the memorial of our redemption,
we remember Christ's Death
and his descent to the realm of the dead,
we proclaim his Resurrection
and his Ascension to your right hand,
and, as we await his coming in glory,
we offer you his Body and Blood,
the sacrifice acceptable to you
which brings salvation to the whole world.

Look, O Lord, upon the Sacrifice
which you yourself have provided for your Church,
and grant in your loving kindness
to all who partake of this one Bread and one Chalice
that, gathered into one body by the Holy Spirit,
they may truly become a living sacrifice in Christ
to the praise of your glory.

Therefore, Lord, remember now
all for whom we offer this sacrifice:
especially your servant N. our Pope,
N. our Bishop,* and the whole Order of Bishops,
all the clergy,
those who take part in this offering,
those gathered here before you,
your entire people,
and all who seek you with a sincere heart.

---

* Mention may be made here of the Coadjutor Bishop, or Auxiliary Bishops.

Meménto étiam illórum,
qui obiérunt in pace Christi tui,
et ómnium defunctórum,
quorum fidem tu solus cognovísti.

Nobis ómnibus, fíliis tuis, clemens Pater, concéde,
ut cæléstem hereditátem cónsequi valeámus
cum beáta Vírgine, Dei Genetríce, María,
cum Apóstolis et Sanctis tuis
in regno tuo, ubi cum univérsa creatúra,
a corruptióne peccáti et mortis liberáta,
te glorificémus per Christum Dóminum nostrum,
per quem mundo bona cuncta largíris.

The Priest takes the chalice and the paten with the host:

Per ipsum, et cum ipso, et in ipso,
est tibi Deo Patri omnipoténti,
in unitáte Spíritus Sancti,
omnis honor et glória
per ómnia sǽcula sæculórum.
R. Amen.
Then follows the Communion Rite, p. 82.

Remember also
those who have died in the peace of your Christ
and all the dead,
whose faith you alone have known.

To all of us, your children,
grant, O merciful Father,
that we may enter into a heavenly inheritance
with the Blessed Virgin Mary, Mother of God,
and with your Apostles and Saints in your kingdom.
There, with the whole of creation,
freed from the corruption of sin and death,
may we glorify you through Christ our Lord,
through whom you bestow on the world all that is good.

The Priest takes the chalice and the paten with the host:

Through him, and with him, and in him,
O God, almighty Father,
in the unity of the Holy Spirit,
all glory and honour is yours,
for ever and ever.

R. Amen.

Then follows the Communion Rite, p. 83.

The Communion Rite

The eating and drinking together of the Lord's Body and Blood in a Paschal meal is the culmination of the Eucharist

The Lord's Prayer

After the chalice and paten have been set down, the congregation stands and the Priest says:

Pr. Præcéptis salutáribus móniti,
et divína institutióne formáti,
audémus dícere:

Together with the people, he continues:

R. **Pater noster, qui es in cælis:
sanctificétur nomen tuum;
advéniat regnum tuum;
fiat volúntas tua, sicut in cælo, et in terra.
Panem nostrum cotidiánum da nobis hódie;
et dimítte nobis debíta nostra,
sicut et nos dimíttimus debitóribus nostris;
et ne nos indúcas in tentatiónem;
sed líbera nos a malo.**

The Communion Rite

The eating and drinking together of the Lord's Body and Blood in a Paschal meal is the culmination of the Eucharist

The Lord's Prayer

After the chalice and paten have been set down, the congregation stands and the Priest says:

Pr. At the Saviour's command
and formed by divine teaching,
we dare to say:

Together with the people, he continues:

R. **Our Father, who art in heaven,
hallowed be thy name;
thy kingdom come,
thy will be done
on earth as it is in heaven.
Give us this day our daily bread,
and forgive us our trespasses,
as we forgive those who trespass against us;
and lead us not into temptation,
but deliver us from evil.**

Pr. Líbera nos, quǽsumus, Dómine, ab ómnibus malis,
da propítius pacem in diébus nostris,
ut, ope misericórdiæ tuæ adiúti,
et a peccáto simus semper líberi
et ab omni perturbatióne secúri:
exspectántes beátam spem
et advéntum Salvatóris nostri Iesu Christi.
R. **Quia tuum est regnum,**
et potéstas, et glória
in sǽcula.

The Peace

Pr. Dómine Iesu Christe, qui dixísti Apostólis tuis:
Pacem relínquo vobis, pacem meam do vobis:
ne respícias peccáta nostra,
sed fidem Ecclésiæ tuæ;
eámque secúndum voluntátem tuam
pacificáre et coadunáre dignéris.
Qui vivis et regnas in sǽcula sæculórum.
R. **Amen.**
Pr. Pax Dómini sit semper vobíscum.
R. **Et cum spíritu tuo.**

Then the Deacon, or the Priest, adds:

Pr. Offérte vobis pacem.
And all offer one another the customary sign of peace.

Pr. Deliver us, Lord, we pray, from every evil,
graciously grant peace in our days,
that, by the help of your mercy,
we may be always free from sin
and safe from all distress,
as we await the blessed hope
and the coming of our Saviour, Jesus Christ.
R. **For the kingdom,**
the power and the glory are yours
now and for ever.

The Peace

Pr. Lord Jesus Christ,
who said to your Apostles:
Peace I leave you, my peace I give you;
look not on our sins,
but on the faith of your Church,
and graciously grant her peace and unity
in accordance with your will.
Who live and reign for ever and ever.
R. **Amen.**
Pr. The peace of the Lord be with you always.
R. **And with your spirit.**

Then the Deacon, or the Priest, adds:

Pr. Let us offer each other the sign of peace.
And all offer one another the customary sign of peace.

Breaking of the Bread

Then the Priest takes the host,.breaks it over the paten, and places a small piece in the chalice, saying quietly:

Pr. Hæc commíxtio Córporis et Sánguinis
Dómini nostri Iesu Christi
fiat accipiéntibus nobis in vitam ætérnam.

Meanwhile the following is sung or said:

Agnus Dei, qui tollis peccáta mundi:
miserére nobis.
Agnus Dei, qui tollis peccáta mundi:
miserére nobis.
Agnus Dei, qui tollis peccáta mundi:
dona nobis pacem.

Invitation to Communion

All kneel. The Priest genuflects, takes the host and, holding it slightly raised above the paten or above the chalice says aloud:

Pr. Ecce Agnus Dei, ecce qui tollit peccáta mundi.
Beáti qui ad cenam Agni vocáti sunt.

R. Dómine, non sum dignus, ut intres sub tectum meum, sed tantum dic verbo, et sanábitur ánima mea.

While the Priest is receiving the Body of Christ, the Communion Chant begins.

Breaking of the Bread

Then the Priest takes the host, breaks it over the paten, and places a small piece in the chalice, saying quietly:

Pr. May this mingling of the Body and Blood
of our Lord Jesus Christ
bring eternal life to us who receive it.

Meanwhile the following is sung or said:

Lamb of God, you take away the sins of the world,
have mercy on us.
Lamb of God, you take away the sins of the world,
have mercy on us.
Lamb of God, you take away the sins of the world,
grant us peace.

Invitation to Communion

All kneel. The Priest genuflects, takes the host and, holding it slightly raised above the paten or above the chalice says aloud:

Pr. Behold the Lamb of God,
behold him who takes away the sins of the world.
Blessed are those called to the supper of the Lamb.

R. Lord, I am not worthy
that you should enter under my roof,
but only say the word
and my soul shall be healed.

While the Priest is receiving the Body of Christ, the Communion Chant begins.

Communion Procession

After the priest has reverently consumed the Body and Blood of Christ he takes the paten or ciborium and approaches the communicants.

The Priest raises a host slightly and shows it to each of the communicants, saying:

Pr. Corpus Christi.

R. Amen.

When Communion is ministered from the chalice the minister offers it to each communicant saying:

Pr. Sanguis Christi.

R. Amen.

After the distribution of Communion, if appropriate, a sacred silence may be observed for a while, or a psalm or other canticle of praise or a hymn may be sung. Then, the Priest says:

Pr. Orémus.

Prayer after Communion

All stand and pray in silence for a while, unless silence has just been observed. Then the Priest says the Prayer after Communion, at the end of which the people acclaim:

R. Amen.

Communion Procession

After the priest has reverently consumed the Body and Blood of Christ he takes the paten or ciborium and approaches the communicants.

The Priest raises a host slightly and shows it to each of the communicants, saying:

Pr. The Body of Christ.

R. Amen.

When Communion is ministered from the chalice the minister offers it to each communicant saying:

Pr. The Blood of Christ.

R. Amen.

After the distribution of Communion, if appropriate, a sacred silence may be observed for a while, or a psalm or other canticle of praise or a hymn may be sung. Then, the Priest says:

Pr. Let us pray.

Prayer after Communion

All stand and pray in silence for a while, unless silence has just been observed. Then the Priest says the Prayer after Communion, at the end of which the people acclaim:

R. Amen.

The Concluding Rites

The Mass closes sending the people forth to put what they have celebrated into effect in their daily lives.

Any brief announcements follow here. Then the dismissal takes place.

Pr. Dóminus vóbiscum.

R. Et cum spíritu tuo.

The Priest blesses the people, saying:

Pr. Benedícat vos omnípotens Deus,
Pater, et Fílius, ✠ et Spíritus Sanctus.

R. Amen.

Then the Deacon, or the Priest himself says the Dismissal:

Pr. Ite, missa est.

R. Deo grátias.

Or:

Pr. Ite, ad Evangélium Dómini annuntiándum.

R. Deo grátias.

Or:

Pr. Ite in pace, glorificándo vita vestra Dóminum.

R. Deo grátias.

Or:

Pr. Ite in pace.

R. Deo grátias.

Then the Priest venerates the altar as at the beginning. After making a profound bow with the ministers, he withdraws.

The Concluding Rites

The Mass closes sending the people forth to put what they have celebrated into effect in their daily lives.

Any brief announcements follow here. Then the dismissal takes place.

Pr. The Lord be with you.

R. And with your spirit.

The Priest blesses the people, saying:

Pr. May almighty God bless you,
the Father, and the Son, ✠ and the Holy Spirit.

R. Amen.

Then the Deacon, or the Priest himself says the Dismissal:

Pr. Go forth, the Mass is ended.

R. Thanks be to God.

Or:

Pr. Go and announce the Gospel of the Lord.

R. Thanks be to God.

Or:

Pr. Go in peace, glorifying the Lord by your life.

R. Thanks be to God.

Or:

Pr. Go in peace.

R. Thanks be to God.

Then the Priest venerates the altar as at the beginning. After making a profound bow with the ministers, he withdraws.

THE MEMORARE

Remember, O most gracious Virgin Mary, that never was it known that anyone who fled to your protection, implored your help or sought your intercession, was left unaided. Inspired by this confidence, I fly unto you, O Virgin of virgins, my Mother. To you I come, before you I stand, sinful and sorrowful. O Mother of the Word incarnate, despise not my petitions, but, in your mercy, hear and answer me. Amen.